DISCARD

Please do not attempt to repair
damages. Alert the library

AFGHANISTAN

Big Buddy Books
An Imprint of Abdo Publishing
abdopublishing.com

Julie Murray

abdopublishing.com

Published by Abdo Publishing, a division of ABDO, PO Box 398166, Minneapolis, Minnesota 55439.
Copyright © 2016 by Abdo Consulting Group, Inc. International copyrights reserved in all countries. No part
of this book may be reproduced in any form without written permission from the publisher. Big Buddy Books™
is a trademark and logo of Abdo Publishing.

Printed in the United States of America, North Mankato, Minnesota.
092015
012016

Cover Photo: Religious Images/UIG/Getty Images.
Interior Photos: ASSOCIATED PRESS (p. 11); Daniel Berehulak/Getty Images (p. 35); Andrew Burton/Getty
    Images (p. 19); DEA/R. FERRANTE/Getty Images (p. 35); Eric Dragesco/NPL/Minden Pictures (p. 23);
    Eye Ubiquitous/Getty Images (p. 35); Sean Gallup/Getty Images (p. 27); Robert Harding/Glow Images
    (pp. 9, 34); © iStockphoto.com (pp. 5, 23); © ITAR-TASS Photo Agency/Alamy (p. 17); JANGIR/AFP/
    Getty Images (p. 11); Aref Karimi/AFP/Getty Images (p. 34); Keystone-France/Getty Images (p. 33);
    WAKIL KOHSAR/AFP/Getty Images (p. 29); Mansell/The LIFE Picture Collection/Getty Images (p. 13);
    SHAH MARAI/AFP/Getty Images (pp. 15, 25); Daniele Pellegrini/Science Source (p. 21); Science &
    Society Picture Library/Getty Images (p. 16); Shutterstock.com (pp. 13, 19, 31, 38); Jerome Starkey/Getty
    Images (p. 37).

Coordinating Series Editor: Megan M. Gunderson
Editor: Katie Lajiness
Contributing Editor: Marcia Zappa
Graphic Design: Adam Craven

Country population and area figures taken from the CIA World Factbook.

Library of Congress Cataloging-in-Publication Data

Murray, Julie, 1969-
  Afghanistan / Julie Murray.
     pages cm -- (Explore the countries.)
  Includes index.
  ISBN 978-1-68078-065-9
  1. Afghanistan--Juvenile literature. I. Title.
  DS351.5.M87 2016
  958.1--dc23
                                        2015026214

AFGHANISTAN

CONTENTS

AROUND THE WORLD

Our world has many countries. Each country has beautiful land. It has its own rich history. And, the people have their own languages and ways of life.

Afghanistan is a country in Asia. What do you know about Afghanistan? Let's learn more about this place and its story!

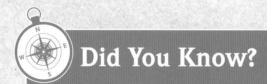

Did You Know?

Pashto and Afghan Persian, or Dari, are official languages in Afghanistan.

Many people think of Afghanistan as hot and dry. But, snow is common in many areas during the winter.

Passport to Afghanistan

Afghanistan shares borders with six countries. It is a landlocked country. So, no bodies of water border it. Afghanistan's total area is 251,827 square miles (652,230 sq km). More than 32 million people live there.

WHERE IN THE WORLD?

UZBEKISTAN

TAJIKISTAN

TURKMENISTAN

CHINA

IRAN

AFGHANISTAN

PAKISTAN

IMPORTANT CITIES

Kabul is Afghanistan's **capital** and largest city, with about 3.4 million people. It has been a city for more than 3,500 years!

Kabul is a mix of old and new buildings. Many buildings were harmed during conflict. And, they have since been rebuilt. The city has businesses that produce food, furniture, and wool.

Did You Know?

Just over 25 percent of Afghan people live in cities. In the United States and Canada, more than 80 percent of people live in cities!

SAY IT

Kabul
KAH-buhl

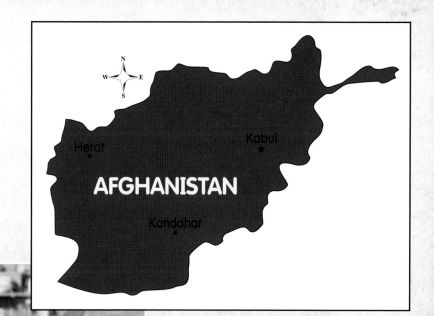

AFGHANISTAN

Herat

Kabul

Kandahar

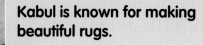

Kabul is known for making beautiful rugs.

Herat is another of Afghanistan's large cities, with about 450,000 people. Its Hari Rud River is part of ancient trade **routes**. These paths went from China to western Asia and Europe. The routes helped Herat grow and gain wealth.

Kandahar is another major city in Afghanistan. It is home to more than 409,000 people. This area is known for growing pomegranates, grapes, and melons. A lot of wool and cotton is produced in Kandahar.

SAY IT

Herat
heh-RAHT

Kandahar
KUHN-duh-hahr

Herat has many bazaars. They have lots of little shops selling different goods.

SAY IT

bazaars
buh-ZAHRS

Kandahar was harmed by many years of war. So, much of the city has been rebuilt.

AFGHANISTAN IN HISTORY

Throughout history, Afghanistan has been in many battles. Several rulers took over ancient Afghanistan from about 1500 to 300 BC.

Then **Muslim** rulers took over Kabul around AD 870. They came from the nearby kingdom of Persia, which is now known as Iran. Muslim kingdoms ruled the area for hundreds of years.

During the 1800s, the British and the Russians both fought for control of Afghanistan. The Afghans fought hard for independence. They gained it in 1919.

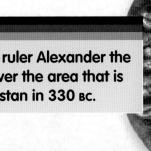

Macedonian ruler Alexander the Great took over the area that is now Afghanistan in 330 BC.

Great Britain and Afghanistan fought three wars from 1839 to 1919.

In 1996, the Taliban took over most of Afghanistan. This group established a new society based on **Islamic** law. The United States and other countries sent military forces to Afghanistan. They overcame the Taliban in 2001.

Concern about the Taliban remained in Afghanistan. To help keep Afghans safe, **foreign** soldiers were still in Afghanistan in 2015. The US military trained Afghan troops to continue on with long-term peace efforts.

Afghanistan's military includes the Afghan National Army and the Afghan Air Force.

15

TIMELINE

1200s

Mongol leader Genghis Khan and his armies took over what is now Afghanistan. Many people were killed when Khan attacked the area.

1925

The afghani was first used as the country's form of money. Before this, Afghanistan used the rupee.

1880

A contract gave Great Britain control over Afghanistan's foreign affairs. But, the British let Afghans control their own government.

1933

Mohammad Zahir Shah became the last king of Afghanistan. He was removed from power and left the country in 1973. Zahir Shah returned in 2002, but he was no longer king.

1979

The Soviet Union sent soldiers to help the liberal Afghan government. They worried that a group of Afghans called the mujahideen might overthrow it. After about nine years of fighting, the mujahideen did overthrow the government in 1992.

2012

Many countries agreed to give 16 billion dollars to help the people in Afghanistan. The money helped the government build more peaceful communities.

An Important Symbol

Afghanistan has had many different flags since the 1900s. Its current flag has three vertical stripes. They are black, red, and green. The flag also has a picture of a **mosque** in the middle.

Afghanistan's government is an **Islamic republic**. The president is the chief of state and head of government.

Afghanistan is divided into 34 provinces. A province is a large section within a country, like a state.

SAY IT

mosque
MAHSK

The current Afghan flag was authorized in 2004.

Ashraf Ghani became president of Afghanistan in 2014. Presidents serve for five years.

SAY IT

Ashraf Ghani
ASH-raf GAH-nee

Did You Know?

Afghanistan has two vice presidents.

Across the Land

Afghanistan has mountains, deserts, valleys, and plains. The Hindu Kush mountain range is 500 miles (800 km) long. The highest peak in Afghanistan is Mount Noshaq. It is about 24,500 feet (7,500 m) high.

 Did You Know?

In January, the average temperature in the northern plains of Afghanistan is about 38°F (3°C). In July, it is about 90°F (32°C).

The Hindu Kush mountain range is the highest in Afghanistan. It runs between central Afghanistan and northern Pakistan.

Few plants grow in southern Afghanistan's deserts. More plants grow in the northern part of the country, which gets more rain. Pine and fir trees grow in the mountains. Some of these trees grow 180 feet (55 m) tall! Roses and honeysuckle grow low in the mountains.

Many types of animals live in Afghanistan. Wolves, wild cats, and gazelles live around the country. Moles, bats, and mongooses occupy less-populated areas.

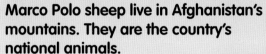

Marco Polo sheep live in Afghanistan's mountains. They are the country's national animals.

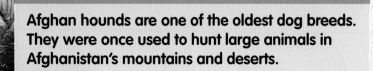

Afghan hounds are one of the oldest dog breeds. They were once used to hunt large animals in Afghanistan's mountains and deserts.

Earning a Living

Many Afghans farm for a living. Most farms are in river valleys. Some farmers dig waterways from rivers to their crops. Common crops include wheat and corn.

In the 1960s, large amounts of natural gas were discovered in Afghanistan. Natural gas comes from the ground. It is used to make electricity. Natural gas brought a lot of money and jobs to the country.

Did You Know?

An afghan is a colorful blanket of knitted or crocheted yarn. The term began because the country has long been known for its beautiful rugs and cloths.

Some farmers are nomads. They move from place to place while their animals find fresh grasses.

LIFE IN AFGHANISTAN

Afghanistan is home to about 20 different groups of people. Most of these groups have their own languages and cultures.

Afghan food is based on the country's main crops and farm animals. Bread is a common food in Afghanistan. People also eat rice with lamb and chicken meat. They eat lots of fruits and vegetables. Dairy foods are also eaten with many meals.

Did You Know?

In Afghanistan, education is free for every child. All children must attend elementary school. The average person receives nine years of education.

Afghans usually eat with their hands. They use bread to scoop up their food.

27

SAY IT

buzkashi
boosh-KUH-shee

Afghanistan's major sport is *buzkashi*. This team sport is played while on horseback. Other popular sports include soccer and wrestling.

Nearly everyone in Afghanistan is **Muslim**. Many people wear **modest** clothes as a sign of their faith. Most Afghan villages have a leader called a mullah. This person leads prayers and teaches young people about the faith.

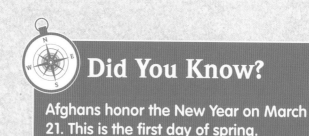

Did You Know?

Afghans honor the New Year on March 21. This is the first day of spring.

Many Afghans gather on Fridays for prayer. Most businesses are closed in honor of this special day.

29

FAMOUS FACES

Rūmī was born around September 30, 1207, in the area that is now Afghanistan. He wrote famous poems in many languages. He wrote in Persian, Arabic, Turkish, and Greek. He died on December 17, 1273.

Many modern people are inspired by Rūmī's poems. He often wrote about love and faith. Many of Rūmī's poems are about his respect for his friend Shams al-Din.

Rūmī's poems are hundreds of years old. Millions of copies are still sold!

SAY IT

Rūmī
ROO-mee

Mohammad Zahir Shah was born on October 15, 1914, in Kabul. He became king of Afghanistan at age 19. He ruled from 1933 to 1973.

Zahir Shah used a lot of **foreign** aid to build up Afghanistan. He had freeways and water pipes built with this money. Zahir Shah died on July 23, 2007.

SAY IT

Mohammad Zahir Shah
moh-HAH-mehd
zah-HEER SHAH

Zahir Shah earned the title of Father of the Nation in Afghanistan.

Tour Book

Imagine traveling to Afghanistan! Here are some places you could go and things you could do.

 ## Learn

Tour the National Museum of Afghanistan. It has items from several thousand years of history.

 ## Travel

Drive Khyber Pass between Afghanistan and Pakistan. This **route** through the mountains has been important throughout history. It served as a path for armies to reach South Asia.

 ## Explore

Visit the Minaret of Jam in central Afghanistan. This tower was once part of a **mosque**. It was used to call people to pray. It is 213 feet (65 m) high! The tower was built around 1190.

Discover

Travel to Babūr's grave in Kabul. See the garden and final resting place of this early ruler.

Relax

Go for a boat ride on Qargha Lake near Kabul. Local people walk around the lake and eat snacks.

A GREAT COUNTRY

The story of Afghanistan is important to our world. Afghanistan is a land of beautiful deserts and mountains. It is a country of strong and talented people.

The people and places that make up Afghanistan offer something special. They help make the world a more beautiful, interesting place.

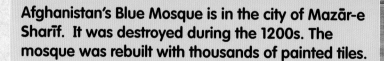

Afghanistan's Blue Mosque is in the city of Mazār-e Sharīf. It was destroyed during the 1200s. The mosque was rebuilt with thousands of painted tiles.

AFGHANISTAN UP CLOSE

Official Name: Islamic Republic of Afghanistan

Flag:

Population (rank): 32,564,342
(July 2015 est.)
(41st most-populated country)

Total Area (rank): 251,827 square miles
(41st largest country)

Capital: Kabul

Official Languages: Afghan Persian (Dari), Pashto

Currency: Afghani

Form of Government: Islamic republic

National Anthem: "Milli Surood"
(National Anthem)

IMPORTANT WORDS

capital a city where government leaders meet.

culture (KUHL-chuhr) the arts, beliefs, and ways of life of a group of people.

foreign coming from or belonging to a different place or country.

inspire to bring about.

Islamic of or relating to Islam, which is a religion based on a belief in Allah as God and Muhammad as his prophet.

liberal believing that the government should be active in supporting social and political change.

modest not showing too much of a person's body.

mosque (MAHSK) a building where Muslims worship.

Muslim a person who practices Islam.

republic a government in which the people choose the leader.

route a road or course that has been traveled, or will be traveled.

WEBSITES

To learn more about Explore the Countries, visit **booklinks.abdopublishing.com**. These links are routinely monitored and updated to provide the most current information available.

INDEX